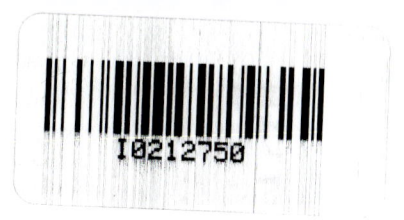

CannaColor: Adult Coloring Book #420

Book: [ISBN# 979-8-218-11442-8]

To request permissions, dm/tweet us @HypotheticalMed or visit:
https://hypotheticalmedical.weebly.com/ask-a-question.html

Table Of Contents:

About CannaColor #420

This is an Adult Coloring book; and we know for many people this may be their first time. For that, we thank you for choosing us; and we promise to make it gentle! Adult coloring books have the same general rules as coloring as a kid: There's no real rules, do whatever you want, and enjoy your time.

You can color in the lines, color outside the lines, use pen, pencil, ink, marker, whatever you'd like. The thicker pages should absorb the various mediums well; and there should be minimal bleed-through for all except thick/heavy markers and some paints. But wait, we show you how to use that to your advantage in the 'bleed-through' frames on the Mandala/Medallion back pages. All the other designs have BLANK Back Pages so that you don't have to worry about bleed-through. If the medium IS bleeding through to the next page; simply rip out the Copyright page and stick it behind your drawing each time, and throw it back into the coloring book as a bookmark so that you always have it.

We made this book with 3 different design types to help you decide how long each session will last:

"QuickHit" Designs - These are our Mandala & Medallion designs and are circular images that can quickly be completed. You can quick-color in 30min for the main design; or you can fill out the details and cover a bit longer session.

"Custom Dabbles" - These custom dabs are for regular sessions. These designs can be completed in an hour or two and are great for a smoke sesh or a relaxing afternoon/evening. These are the main designs in this book; and you might see anything from angular/geometric designs on one page, to a flowing, wavy-line trippy drawing on the next. Logos, Jokes, even CannAnimals – so anything is fair game.

"SlowBurn" Designs - These are designs that take up a full page, usually with many small or intricate designs throughout the piece. You'll either want to kiss us or curse us; but these will take many HOURS to complete… it's designed to take half a day or multiple sessions.

Another cool & unique thing about this coloring book is the encouraged use of different materials to enhance designs. We'll show how to make stuff pop with GILDING LINES, or how to use intentional BLEED-THRU templates to help 'frame' your Mandala designs from the back page marker bleed.

Finally; you'll notice we include some EMOJI's throughout this coloring book; and that will be used for additional things you can do on each design. We'll learn more about those on the next page.

Tips & Tricks

There's some COOL TRICKS to adult coloring books that you might not know about; so we'll give you a short tutorial of some techniques & cool tips.

But first; we recommend grabbing a "Quick HIt" Mandala or Medallion and just try your first image now. We can use this to compare to 'after' you learn some tricks & techniques to see how they help!

Now that you've done a quick design… read & try these below.   Example Coloring Techniques:

✏️ 3D Shading, ⬜ Lighting & ⬛ Shadows - Create depth and motion using using these 3 techniques. A simple shadow makes an object become 3D. Shading, with lighting, creates depth & realism, even motion. Start with a dark color fill, use concentrically lighter colors to reflect an overhead light source.

🖌️ Blending - Create realistic creations by use of subtle changes in color to reflect what an eye would see. Concentric circles with decreasing color creates depth; but blending the lines makes it realistic. Overlap colors, use a light-to-heavier touch with a single color, or even just blend colors with your thumb (on crayon) or eraser (pencil, colored pencils, some pens); or try cotton dipped in alcohol (test 1st)!

✖️ Cross-Hatching & ➖ Hatching - Parallel lines or Intersecting lines to create color with minimal coverage, similar to old comic books & newspaper artwork. It's like shorthand for "this is this color"

🖍️ Gilding Lines - Using a reflective PEN or MARKER; go over our coloring lines or add new ones into a drawing. This hides the lines (so it no longer looks like a coloring book), & makes the image POP. Gold, Chrome, & dark colors work wonders; especially contrasted with colored pencil artwork!

⛔ Negative Space - A reverse-image created within a design. Draw an outline of your image, then color everything OUTSIDE the lines, the inside becomes the focal point. Add words & shapes 🆔 💜

🌀 Scumbling, 🔆 Stippling - This is a drawing technique to fill in similar to Hatching/XHatching but it adds different textures. Scumbling is just a single loopy line turned into endless squiggles, great for filling in things like hair or faraway trees. Stippling is making many points of varying frequency for depth and coloring in.   Example is the skin of an orange, or hair follicles on a close up view.

Notice the Emoji's? We'll sprinkle them in as examples, but don't be afraid to try these tips anywhere!

Drawing Technique Examples

Emojis are sprinkled throughout the coloring book as a good place to try these ideas. Each one is within the design, and at a lighter opacity so they can easily be colored over. We don't want to ruin your artwork, so you'll only see these on a handful of pages. These are a good starting point for your first designs, like practice material. Pages with these icons will have comparatively simple designs and open spaces to experiment; great for the first attempt of these techniques.

Below are some examples of each of our techniques:

■ 3D Shading   □ Lighting   ✏ Shadows   ✏ Blending   🖌 Gilding Lines

✖ Cross-Hatch   ═ Hatching   🌀 Scumbling   ☀ Stippling   ⊖ Negative Space

Technique Legend:
✏ 3D Shading   □ Lighting   ■ Shadows   ✏ Blending   🖌 Gilding Lines
✖ Crosshatching   ═ Hatching   🌀 Scumbling   ☀ Stippling   ⊖ Negative Space

Flyin' High

SMOKE & TOKE

MOTORCYCLE CLUB

Don't Give Me No STATIC

High Maintenance

Vibe With Me

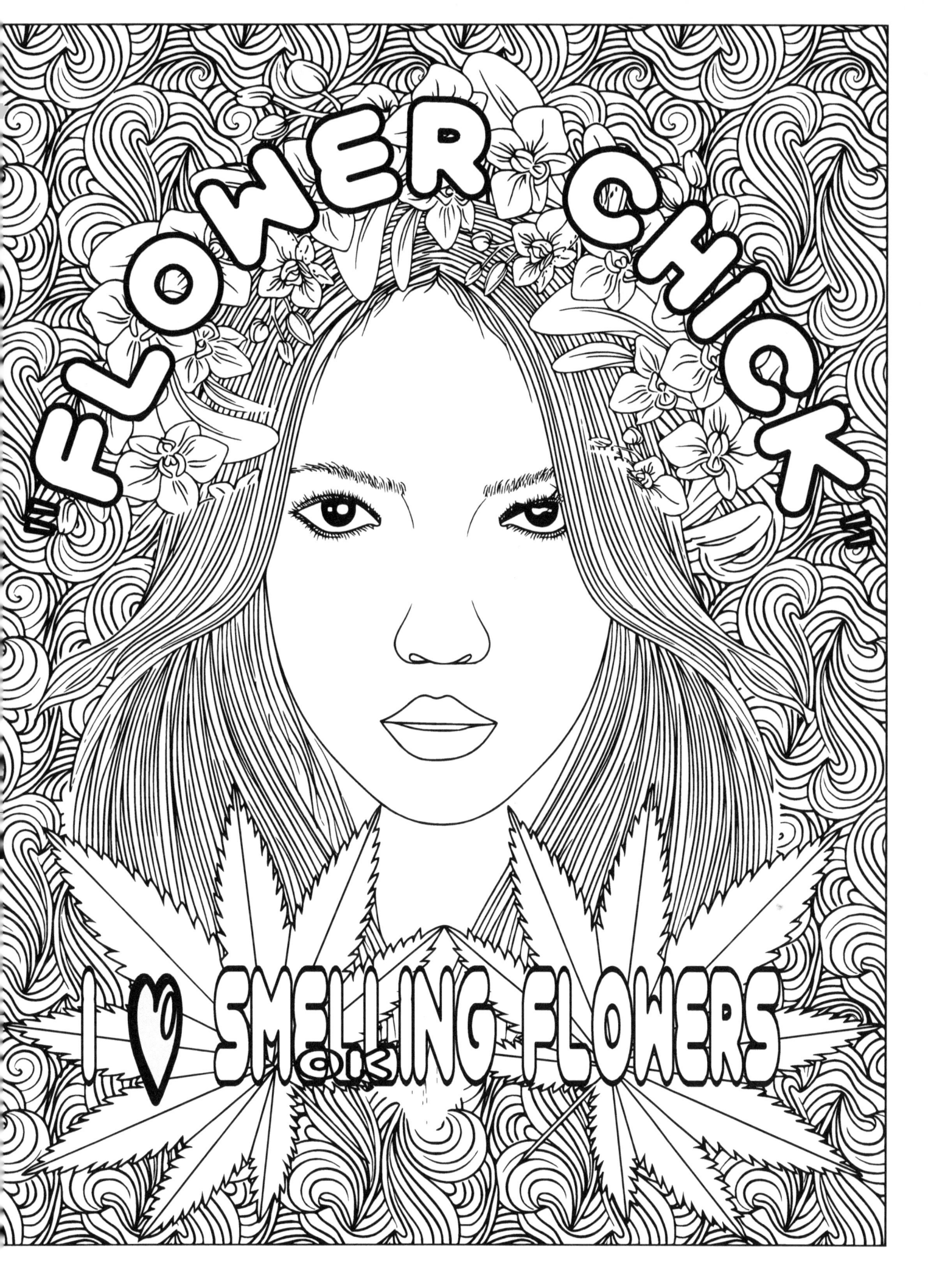

"FLOWER CHICK"

I ♥ SMELLING FLOWERS

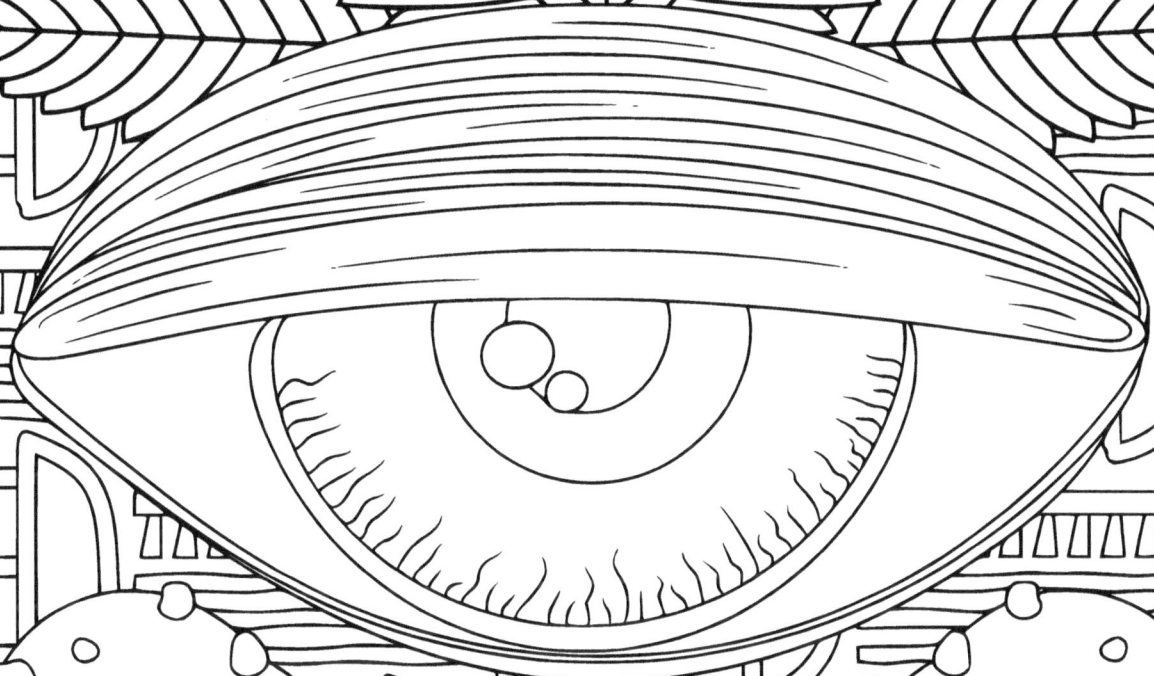

Cannabis - Favorite Strain Type:

CANNANIMAL

HUMAN LAPWARMER

CANNANIMAL

MAN'S BEST FRIEND

WHAT IF YOU TRY TO

Think Like An Egyptian

IN THE HARD TIMES

WE GROW THE MOST

WORLDS DOPEST DAD

LIKE YOUR DAD, ONLY HIGHER

MARIJUANA MAMA

Ain't No Time 4 Drama

Weed Limit 420

WHEN YOU SMOKE THE HERB

It's A Good Time To Color & Stipple

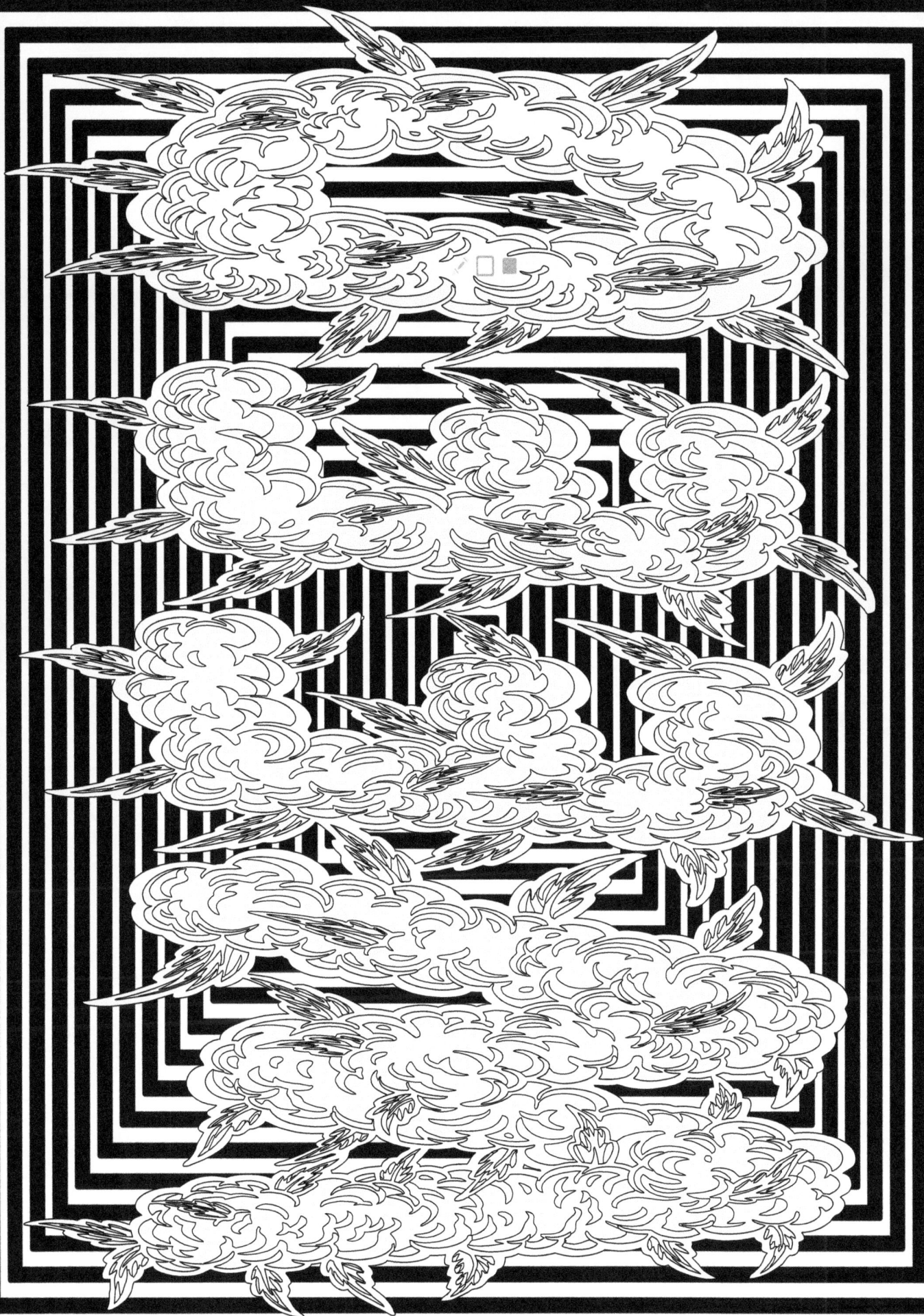

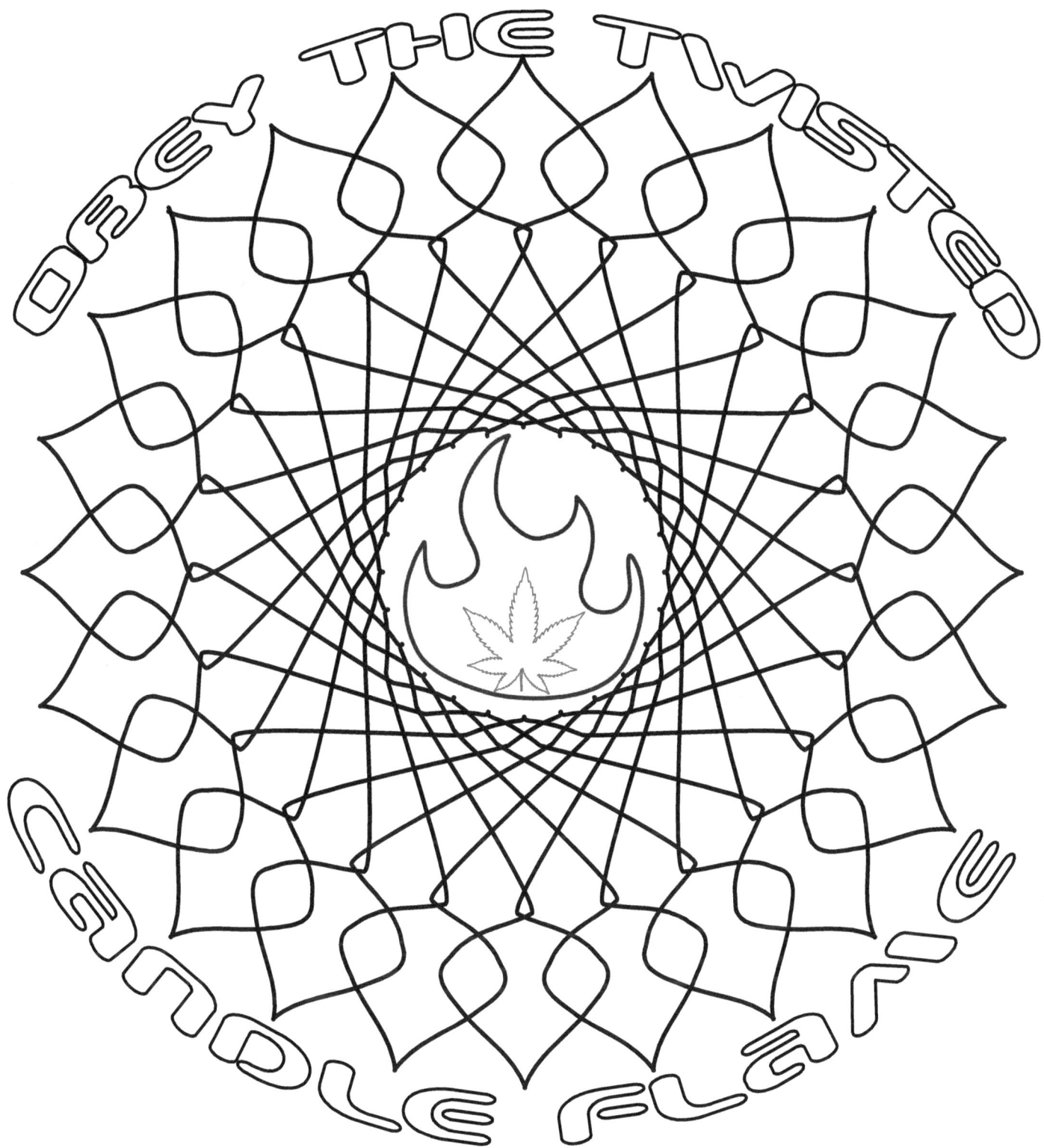

OBEY THE TWISTED

CANDLE FLAME

THESE ARE OUTLINES OF THE NEGATIVE SPACE AREAS
FOR THE DESIGN FROM THE PAGE BEHIND THIS TEXT.

FEEL FREE TO COLOR IN THE AREAS OUTLINED ON THIS PAGE

NOTE: IF YOU USE MARKER OR GEL PEN, IT MIGHT BLEED THROUGH TO
THE OTHER SIDE. SO, IT MIGHT SHOW ON THE REVERSE SIDE IMAGE.

USE THIS TO YOUR ADVANTAGE TO MAKE DARK BLEED-THRU
DESIGNS TO "FRAME" YOUR IMAGE ON REVERSE PAGE!

THESE ARE OUTLINES OF THE NEGATIVE SPACE AREAS
FOR THE DESIGN FROM THE PAGE BEHIND THIS TEXT.

FEEL FREE TO COLOR IN THE AREAS OUTLINED ON THIS PAGE

NOTE: IF YOU USE MARKER OR GEL PEN, IT MIGHT BLEED THROUGH TO
THE OTHER SIDE. SO, IT MIGHT SHOW ON THE REVERSE SIDE IMAGE.

USE THIS TO YOUR ADVANTAGE TO MAKE DARK BLEED-THRU
DESIGNS TO "FRAME" YOUR IMAGE ON REVERSE PAGE!

THESE ARE OUTLINES OF THE NEGATIVE SPACE AREAS
FOR THE DESIGN FROM THE PAGE BEHIND THIS TEXT.

FEEL FREE TO COLOR IN THE AREAS OUTLINED ON THIS PAGE

NOTE: IF YOU USE MARKER OR GEL PEN, IT MIGHT BLEED THROUGH TO
THE OTHER SIDE. SO, IT MIGHT SHOW ON THE REVERSE SIDE IMAGE.

USE THIS TO YOUR ADVANTAGE TO MAKE DARK BLEED-THRU
DESIGNS TO "FRAME" YOUR IMAGE ON REVERSE PAGE!

THESE ARE OUTLINES OF THE NEGATIVE SPACE AREAS
FOR THE DESIGN FROM THE PAGE BEHIND THIS TEXT.

FEEL FREE TO COLOR IN THE AREAS OUTLINED ON THIS PAGE

NOTE: IF YOU USE MARKER OR GEL PEN, IT MIGHT BLEED THROUGH TO
THE OTHER SIDE. SO, IT MIGHT SHOW ON THE REVERSE SIDE IMAGE.

USE THIS TO YOUR ADVANTAGE TO MAKE DARK BLEED-THRU
DESIGNS TO "FRAME" YOUR IMAGE ON REVERSE PAGE!

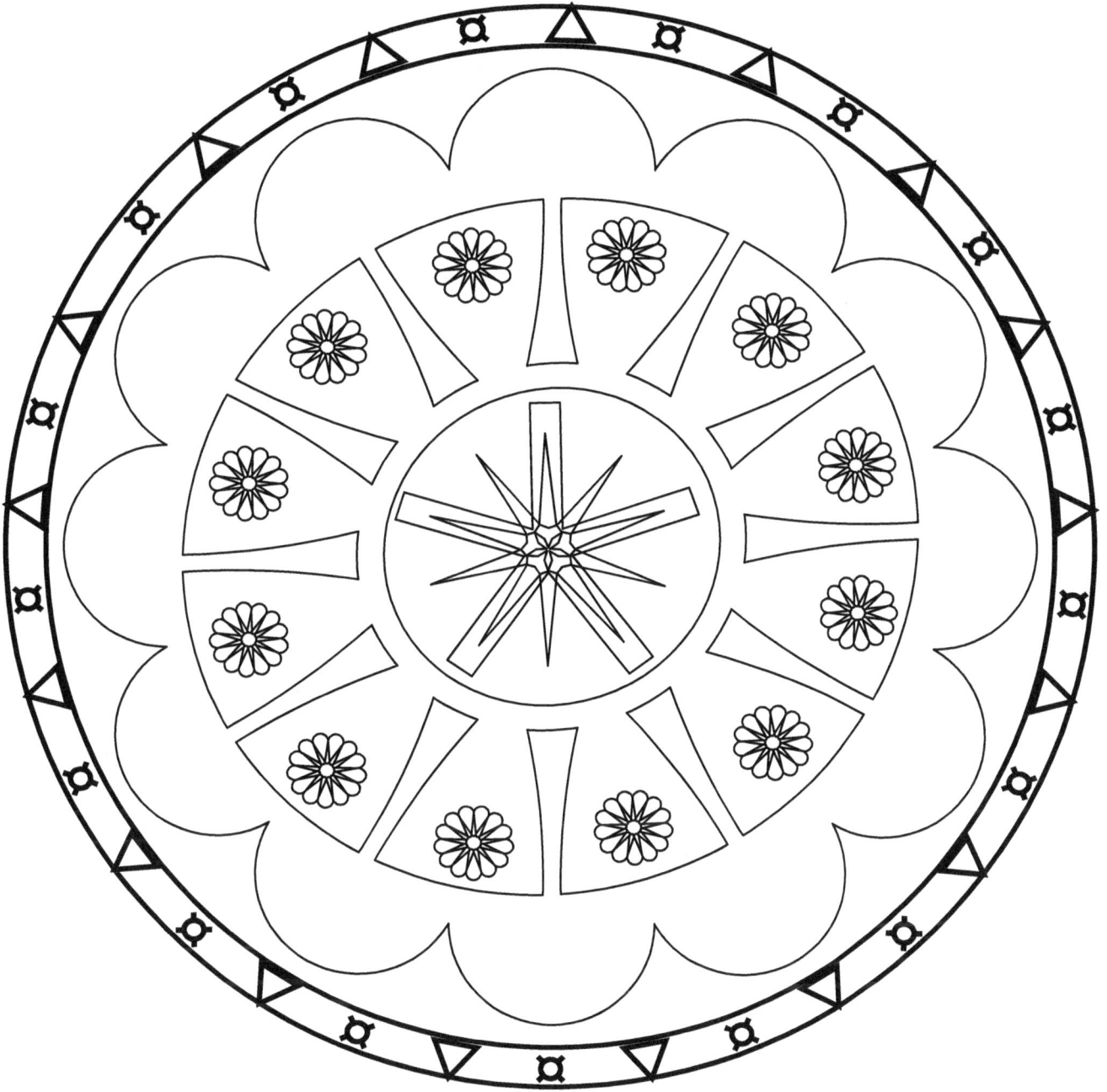

THESE ARE OUTLINES OF THE NEGATIVE SPACE AREAS
FOR THE DESIGN FROM THE PAGE BEHIND THIS TEXT.

FEEL FREE TO COLOR IN THE AREAS OUTLINED ON THIS PAGE

NOTE: IF YOU USE MARKER OR GEL PEN, IT MIGHT BLEED THROUGH TO
THE OTHER SIDE. SO, IT MIGHT SHOW ON THE REVERSE SIDE IMAGE.

USE THIS TO YOUR ADVANTAGE TO MAKE DARK BLEED-THRU
DESIGNS TO "FRAME" YOUR IMAGE ON REVERSE PAGE!

THESE ARE OUTLINES OF THE NEGATIVE SPACE AREAS
FOR THE DESIGN FROM THE PAGE BEHIND THIS TEXT.

FEEL FREE TO COLOR IN THE AREAS OUTLINED ON THIS PAGE

NOTE: IF YOU USE MARKER OR GEL PEN, IT MIGHT BLEED THROUGH TO
THE OTHER SIDE. SO, IT MIGHT SHOW ON THE REVERSE SIDE IMAGE.

USE THIS TO YOUR ADVANTAGE TO MAKE DARK BLEED-THRU
DESIGNS TO "FRAME" YOUR IMAGE ON REVERSE PAGE!

THESE ARE OUTLINES OF THE NEGATIVE SPACE AREAS
FOR THE DESIGN FROM THE PAGE BEHIND THIS TEXT.

FEEL FREE TO COLOR IN THE AREAS OUTLINED ON THIS PAGE

NOTE: IF YOU USE MARKER OR GEL PEN, IT MIGHT BLEED THROUGH TO
THE OTHER SIDE. SO, IT MIGHT SHOW ON THE REVERSE SIDE IMAGE.

USE THIS TO YOUR ADVANTAGE TO MAKE DARK BLEED-THRU
DESIGNS TO "FRAME" YOUR IMAGE ON REVERSE PAGE!

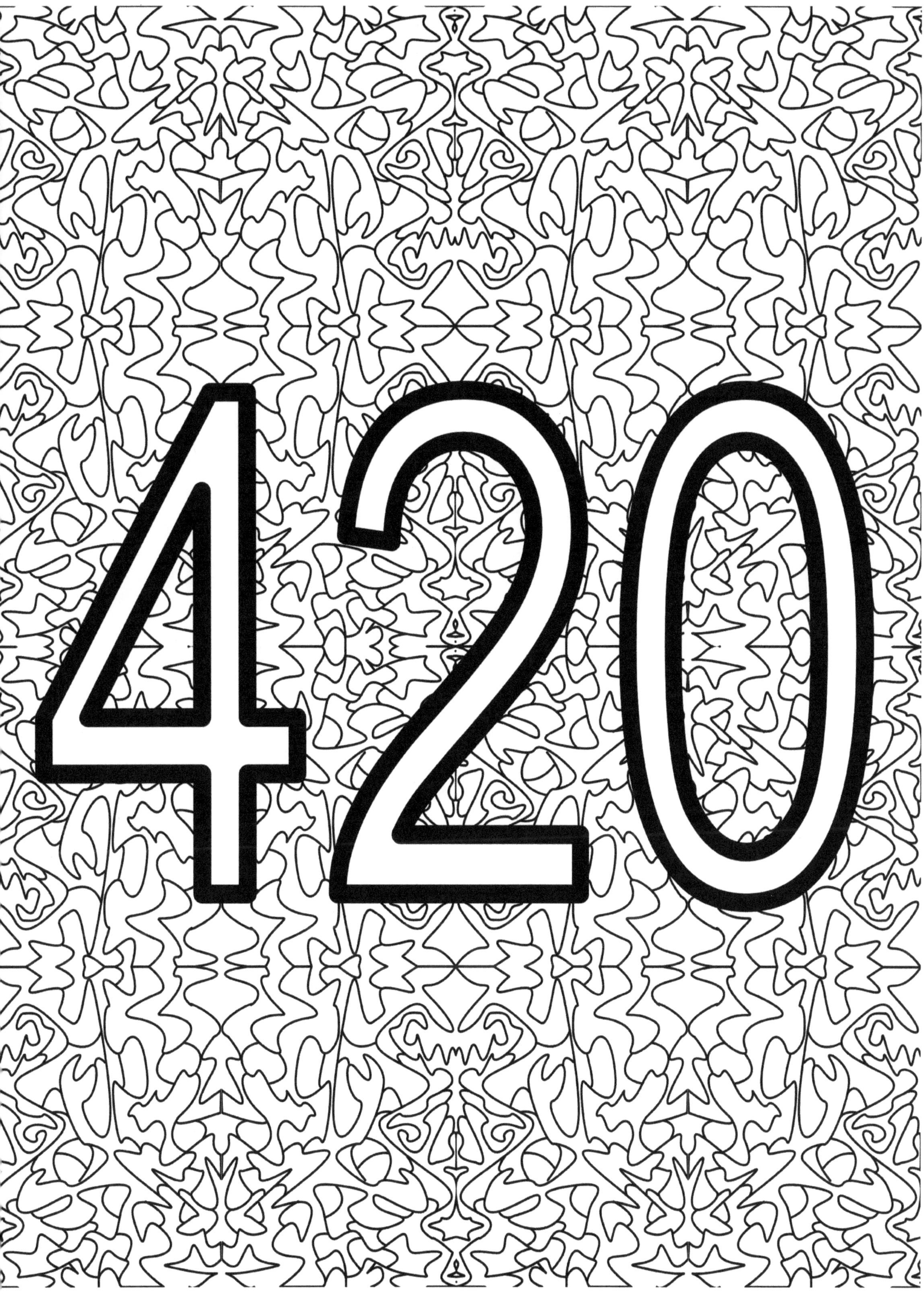
420

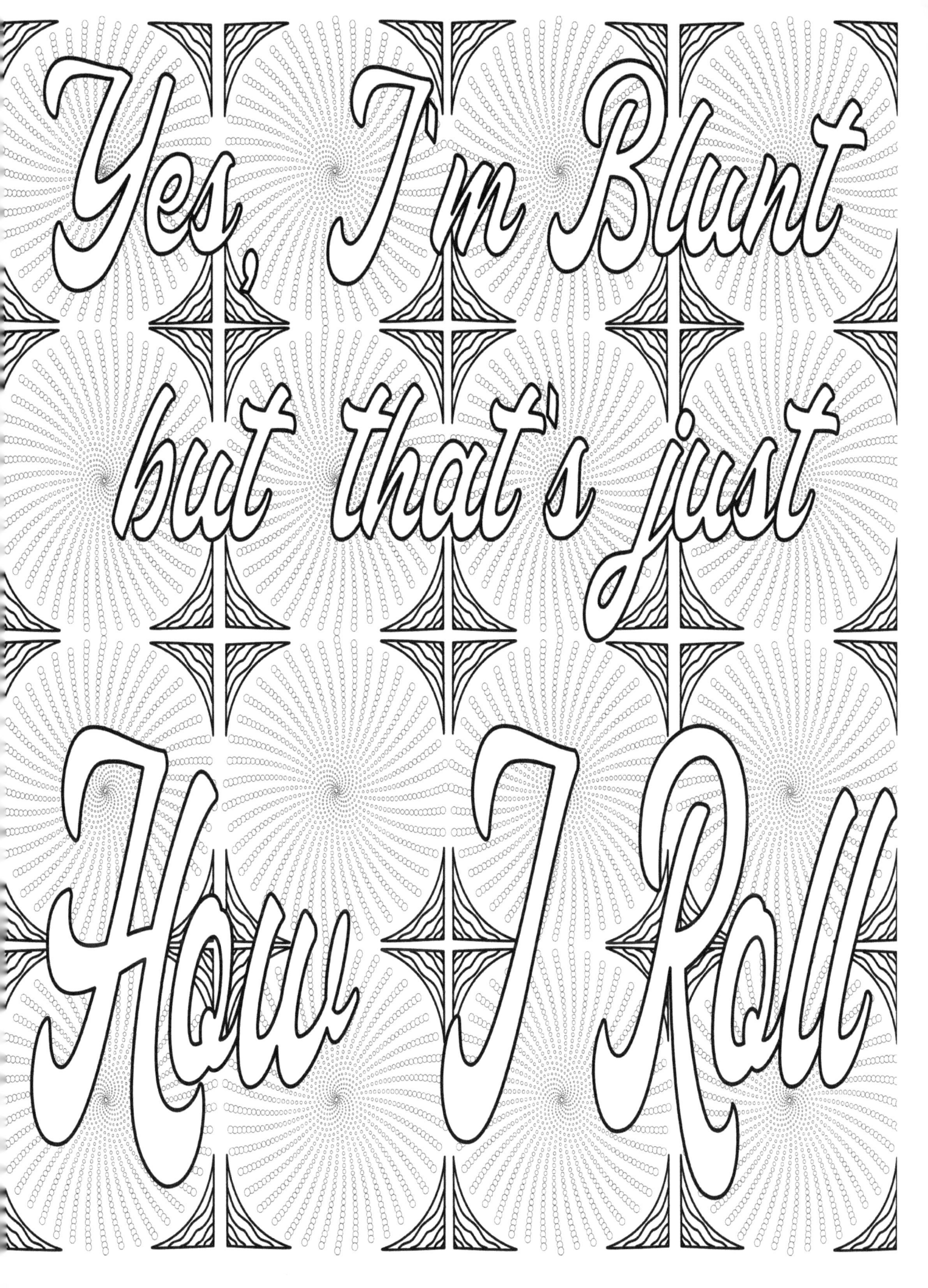

Yes, I'm Blunt but that's just How I Roll

My House To Dank

All The Potatto's Are Baked

INHALE
THE GOOD SHIT
EXHALE
THE BULLSHIT

Some of my Finest Hours have been spent on my back Veranda, Smoking Hemp & observing as far as my eye can see

-Thomas Jefferson

Thank You & Bonus Content

This coloring book was brought to you by H-Med.biz

H-Med: The Hypothetical Medical Co. is an activist brand trying to de-stigmatize smokable medicine. The world witnessed how dangerous a decade of misinformation is; imagine trying to overcome propaganda & misinformation that's been around for NINE DECADES.

Stereotypes like 'reefer madness' crazies, to the 'lazy stoner' tropes are still around today; repeated so often that people think it's true. We're also up against confusing laws, lack of research due to hypocritical regulations, & lack of study results due to these unfair hurdles. There's very little professional educational content available; and responsible adults want to be entertained or enjoy 420 merch without feeling like it's a Taboo subject.

H-Med makes this content for our OCEAN Initiative. We focus on Outreach, Community (engagement), Education, Advocacy, & Normalization content. If you enjoy this coloring book, please visit our YouTube channel. To find out more OR to support us by buying merch (& funding our content); visit https://www. H-Med.biz

Bonus Content:
Have you ever heard of digital coloring? Digital coloring is using various programs on your phone, tablet, or computer creating perfect touch-and-paint art. Instant fill is glorious fast-coloring! No skill necessary, just choose the colors & flourishes you like, no need to worry about coloring in the lines.

We sell this coloring book CannaColor420 as a digital edition on our website. You download the book and can use a program such as Microsoft Paint and use the 'fill' tool to fill in the various parts of the artwork. Great on the Mandala/Medallions and the Slow-Burns… it's the online equivalent of virtually popping packing material bubbles. Fun and simple, mesmerizing, and when finished you'll have something you can share online. To get a FREE copy of the digital version; simply take a completed picture from this book and share it with us on any of our social media or at http://www.H-Med.biz and we will provide a free copy via email.

We want to say thank you. We appreciate you spending your time with us, and we hope you enjoy our creative prompts. We hope you enjoyed this adult coloring book, and can't wait to see the awesome creations you make.

Lastly, please review this book wherever you purchased it from. We really appreciate your review 💟